Acclaim for *Own Your Time*

Stephanie Wachman's book is profound and practical. Any executive will find immediately actionable ideas to improve productivity, all conveyed in a clear and concise fashion.
— JOHN BLACKBURN, PRESIDENT, NET RETURN CAPITAL

"Stephanie Wachman shows how modern tools for success can undermine our lives and productivity when they control us instead of us controlling them. Her book brings to mind the old adage, "How do you eat an elephant? One bite at a time." Wachman doesn't stop there; she provides us with the fork.
— ROBIN JOHNSON, M.D., emergency physician, public health director, mother

"As an overwrought physician, I rarely feel like my time belongs to me. Stephanie Wachman taught me to grab back the reigns of my runaway life. Readable, practical, and economical, Wachman's book offers great advice for busy professionals. From how to politely say no, to running efficient meetings, to prioritizing tasks, she coaches and you reap the rewards."
— TIMOTHY RUMMEL, M.D.

"*Own Your Time* provides time-management solutions for problems that executives and managers face every day. Stephanie Wachman addresses today's time stealers, such as social media and email. It's an easy read that gets straight to the point."
— MIKE BERGER, Senior Broker Associate, Weichert Realtors

Own Your Time

Own Your Time

PROFESSIONAL TIME-MANAGEMENT STRATEGIES
FOR A PROFITABLE AND BALANCED LIFE

Stephanie Wachman

Life in Balance, LLC
Denver, Colorado

Life in Balance, LLC
Denver, Colorado
www.stephaniewachman.com

First Edition: October 2016

ISBN Print Version: 978-0-9977961-0-0
ISBN Ebook: 978-0-9977961-1-7

Cover Design: Rebecca Finkle

1. Business 2. Time-Management

Printed in the United States of America

CONTENTS

About the Author

STEPHANIE WACHMAN is a Fortune 500 executive coach and time-management expert. Her clients include companies such as FedEx, KPMG, Ingram Micro, Level 3 Communications, and University of Colorado Hospital, as well as national private equity and law firms. She is past-president of the Colorado chapter of the International Coach Federation.

Prior to starting her executive coaching business, Life in Balance, LLC, Wachman worked for more than twenty years as a sales executive. A dedicated parent, she knows the daily tensions that business professionals face as they compete in the global marketplace while sustaining healthy families and friendships.

Wachman studied executive coaching with Coach Training Alliance, ISEI, Judy Sabah, *New York Times* best-selling author Shirzad Chamine, and Steve Mitten, a master certified coach. A graduate of McGill University in Canada, Wachman lives with her husband and two children in Denver.

Acknowledgments

Writing this book has been a true labor of love. During my years in the corporate world, I worked late hours and traveled extensively. At that time, I didn't understand the time-management practices in this book. As a result, I missed a lot of time at home with my family, which was extremely difficult and painful. My goal is to help others avoid what I endured.

So this book is dedicated to all the men and women who are exhausted, stressed, and on the verge of burnout. I thank you for providing me with the opportunity to help you find more balance in your life. I hope this book provides the solutions you need without having to read a tome.

I am also grateful for my editor, Glenn McMahan. His encouragement and dedication helped me bring this book into the world.

All importantly, I thank my family—David, Joshua, and Ben—for their continued love and support.

*There is more to life
than increasing its speed.*

— Mahatma Ghandi

OWN YOUR TIME

CHAPTER 1

THE TIME OF YOUR LIFE

TIME IS THE GREAT EQUALIZER. Everyone has the same amount of time each day. What makes the difference is how we choose to manage our time. Use it poorly and you will face increased stress, depleted energy, and missed opportunities. Use it wisely, and you can find a healthy balance between rest, family, work, and wealth. In many regards, daily choices are about time management—what we do with our lives!

As I reviewed numerous time-management books, I found that many authors theorize from thirty thousand feet above the fray. They assume that if you write a personal mission statement, set the right goals, and use a cool scheduling app, then all will be well.

It's not that easy in workplace trenches. Personal mission statements don't help when you're coping with a hundred emails, Internet distractions, moody kids who didn't finish homework, and your own tendency to procrastinate. Plans? Goals? Right . . .

It's also clear that business professionals are desperate for on-the-ground help. In 2013, as reported in the *The Wall Street Journal,* the consulting firm McKinsey & Co. surveyed fourteen hundred senior executives from the public and private sector about time management. Only 9 percent said they were "highly satisfied" with the way they were using their time at work. One author of the report concluded that, "Time is one of the most precious and under-managed resources at a company, and it seems to be getting more so." Obviously, the lack of time-management skills is hurting profits.

Time-management problems at work inevitably spill into our personal lives. According to a 2011 report by the American Psychological Association, about half of all American professionals say they don't have a healthy life balance. Nearly 40 percent of workers surveyed say they are extremely stressed. This is true not only in the U.S., but also in every developed nation.

For managers, leaders, business professionals, and CEOs, time management directly impacts individual performance and company profits. Yet today we face an increasing number of demands on our schedules even though our time is finite. This situation, which is not likely to change, means that we must do a better job of managing our time. That is the only way we can regain control of our lives.

I am a working mother. In my previous career, before I learned to manage my time well, I always felt torn between work and family. I felt like I never had enough time with my kids. I was managing hundreds of sales people and traveling across the country every week. Whenever I was with my family, I was never completely present and I always felt guilty because my mind was always on my work. I learned that managing my time, both at work and at home, was critical for my long-term well-being and my family's, too.

Time means different things at different phases of our lives and careers. When we're young we feel like we have all the time in the world. As we get older and have families, all the competing priorities make us feel like we never have enough time. A person with a serious illness will find that time is even more precious. In fact, when I was forty-three years old, I was diagnosed with breast cancer. I had two young children and I had already made a shift in careers to executive coaching in order spend more time with my husband and kids. I can't find words to express how precious time became to me as I went through that hard season. Time continues to be a valuable commodity even though I am in remission.

We don't know what's around the corner in life. This makes time management matter even more. It's about how we live our lives. So don't take the strategies in this book lightly.

If you are struggling to regain balance in your life, this book will help you make long-term and progressive change. As you put these solutions into practice, the weight of the world that sits on your shoulders will begin to decrease. You will begin to feel lighter, more hopeful, and happier.

Time management is a skill that should not take a lot of time to learn! That's why this book is short. Each chapter provides tips and strategies that you can use to improve your productivity. You can start by incorporating one or two ideas and exercises into your routine. After you've mastered those, work on a couple more. By practicing the strategies in the book for a while, you will be able to measure your progress.

I encourage you to use this book as your time-management desk reference. When you start to feel overwhelmed, distracted, stressed, exhausted, or anxious, you can go back to a specific chapter and re-establish a positive strategy. When you find you've forgotten a time-management skill, this book will be nearby to help you remember.

You can take a time-management quiz at my website (www.stephaniewachman.com). It will show you where you need help and give you a baseline from which to measure progress. After reading the book and practicing my strategies, you can take the quiz again to see how you've improved.

Own Your Time is about taking control of your time and understanding what you need to do to achieve a healthy life balance. The truth is, it is very difficult to get balance in our lives. But if you practice the techniques and strategies in this book you will be more productive, feel less stressed, improve your relationships, and enjoy more of life—all at the same time.

CHAPTER 2

THE WHY OF PROCRASTINATION

I PUT OFF WRITING THIS CHAPTER about procrastination for a long time despite the fact that this was one of the topics I wanted to tackle first. We all struggle with the "I'll do it later" syndrome. We never lack reasons to put things off until another day, month, or year.

The Procrastination Research Group at Carleton University in Canada did an online survey about this tendency. They received twenty-seven hundred responses to the following question: "To what extent is procrastination having a negative impact on your happiness?" Almost one person in two (46 percent) said "quite a bit" or "very much." Around one person in five (18 percent) reported an "extreme negative effect."

This has been true at times in my career. I once had a job that required me to make more than two hundred telephone cold calls a week. Over the course of seven years, I logged about seventy-six thousand calls. This was the least exciting part of my job. I consistently put it off. As a result, my sales numbers began to slump, as did my confidence and happiness. This led to a downward spiral. The less confident I became, the more I resisted picking up the phone. That resulted in even less self-confidence. I began to feel awful about myself. Then I had to present my weak sales numbers to the company leadership, and the only excuse was my procrastination. I simply didn't feel like making the calls. Something had to change or I would be out of a job.

I realized that I needed to figure out why I kept procrastinating. I searched for a better understanding of my behavior. First, I realized that I anticipated frequent rejection to my sales calls, which I hated. This caused me to put off the work, which in turn led to failure. Second, it became clear that I didn't know where to start when facing such a daunting list of calls.

The way I overcame procrastination, in this instance, was to look ahead at the results I really wanted to achieve and to use that vision as my motivation. I wanted to keep my job, I wanted to blow my sales quota out of the water, and I wanted the commission that came with good sales. Once I was clear about what I wanted, then I had to ask myself the question, "What do I absolutely need to do to achieve the outcomes I want?" The answer was to *make the calls*. I put my desire for success in the driver's seat and pushed my fear of rejection to the back. In regard to feeling overwhelmed by the huge number of calls, I decided to break the list down into manageable chunks of forty calls per day. Taking small bites was easier than eating the whole elephant. I was then able to start working to achieve some positive results.

In truth, I still didn't enjoy making those calls. Some were very uncomfortable to make. One time I dialed a number only to find out that the person I tried to call had left the company years earlier. That was embarrassing, especially since I had to continue prospecting on that same call. But after overcoming my procrastination and keeping to my schedule, I won an award for record sales.

Procrastination is a common tendency. It is a way to protect ourselves from something uncomfortable. Fear might be the main cause of procrastination. By avoiding what makes us uncomfortable we don't have to deal with it. And because we are so easily distracted, it's far more comforting to fill the time with something else, such as surfing the Internet, watching bad reality shows, or text messaging. Without a clear strategic goal for what we want to accomplish, we will allow distractions and excuses to sabotage our success.

SILENCING THE INNER CRITIC

Coaching professionals have identified another common cause of procrastination. It is called the voice of the *saboteur*, or the voice of the inner critic. Every client I have ever worked with has had challenges with their inner critic. This voice in our head causes people to constantly find fault in themselves, even if they are highly successful. It can cause low self-esteem. Our inner critic undermines self-confidence. This may sound a bit "out there" to those of you who have never experienced it, but it is real.

Here are some of the most common sayings from the inner critics of my clients:

"You're too lazy, disorganized, and uncreative to ever be able to do that work."

"You don't know anything about . . ."

"It'll never happen no matter how hard you try."

"Sure, you landed two new clients yesterday, but you should have landed three. How on earth did you blow that? You are going to be found out as a fraud."

The inner critic likes to hang out in our subconscious mind waiting to pounce at any moment of insecurity. It causes us to be controlled by fear of failure, fear of being laughed at, and fear of being wrong. Excessive negative thinking can cause the body to produce more cortisol, which can make us more irritable and discouraged.

I have found through my work that many business professionals fear their work doesn't make a difference in the company. The inner critic tells them that they don't matter, which in turn saps motivation and leads to more procrastination.

To compensate for the inner critic, we often occupy ourselves with useless distractions and invent fake excuses. These rationalizations satisfy the *saboteur* but wreak havoc with our personal power and prevent us from focusing on what we need to do to be successful.

There are effective ways to counter the attacks of the inner critic, and if you have a sense of humor, these methods can be fun.

First, I recommend drawing a picture of what you imagine your inner critic looks like, as if it were a cartoon character. You don't have to be an artist; just draw it. Next, give your *saboteur* a name and make a list of all the nasty things it likes to say. For example, I had a client who named his critic Buzz Kill. This *saboteur* liked to tell my client that he couldn't do anything right, that he was a fake, and that he should have no expectations for future success.

Once you've "humanized" your inner critic, you can employ techniques to shut it up. You'll never get rid of it, but you can quiet its voice from a scream to a whisper. I had a client who put her inner critic in "time out" every time the voice of negativity popped into her head. Another client would give the voice sixty seconds to rattle on every morning. Then she refused to pay attention to the voice for the rest of the day. Another client bought a bird cage and every time he started to beat himself up he would write down what his inner critic was saying and put the list in the cage.

The best way to deal with the inner critic is to be aware of it and ask yourself: Is what my inner critic saying true? Am I really a fraud? Am I always wrong? You get the idea. You can be honest about your short-comings—we all have them—but those should not lead us to believe we have no future. Remind yourself that your *saboteur* tells lies. Your mind is powerful, so don't let the *saboteur* be your business manager.

There are two fantastic books that go deeper into dealing with the inner critic. They are titled *Taming Your Gremlin,* by Rick Carson, and *Positive Intelligence,* by Shirzad Chamine. If this is a recurring challenge in your life, causing you to procrastinate or feel down about yourself, then these books offer great tools to deal with it.

SIX WAYS TO OVERCOME PROCRASTINATION

1. Be aware. Once we understand our tendency to procrastinate, it's easy to address the problem. List the causes of your procrastination and then build a strategy for overcoming them. For example, while writing this book I kept postponing the work. I didn't have a clue where to start. So I built a schedule. I decided to write about one topic for two hours each day over three months. That's all it took. I had a plan that was simple but strategic in helping me achieve my goal. So ask yourself: Why you are procrastinating and what strategy can you build to achieve your goals?

2. Divide tasks into manageable parts. Remember my example of breaking down two hundred phone calls to forty per day for five days? If you are feeling overwhelmed by everything you need to do, divide all the tasks into smaller parts and tackle one at a time. Success with one task will help you feel encouraged to work on the others. Brian Tracy, in his book on productivity, *Eat That Frog*, suggests doing what you dislike first so you can focus on the work you enjoy. That doesn't work for everybody. Sometimes it's more effective to conquer the smaller, more manageable tasks first. This gives you a feeling of accomplishment and helps you get on a roll. I recommend using whichever technique fits you best. The key is to make sure that you break tasks down so they are manageable. Otherwise they will loom large over your head, weigh you down, and clutter your mind.

3. Prioritize. Setting good priorities will help you avoid feeling overwhelmed. Work on the most important tasks first. Use the Eisenhower Matrix, described in chapter 12, to help you prioritize your task list. This matrix is a tool that can help you figure which tasks are important, urgent, unimportant, and non-urgent.

4. Set a timer. For those tasks that you don't want to do, set a timer and try to finish them before time runs out. This will keep you motivated and focused.

5. Remove unnecessary tasks. Take a close look at your list of tasks and ask if they are all worth your time and effort. You will find that many tasks don't need to be on your list. Removing them will help you feel less overwhelmed by the workload.

6. Get your schedule organized. If you procrastinate because you're disorganized, there are some powerful ways to develop a more organized agenda. I will address more about scheduling and priorities in future chapters, but for now you can improve your scheduling abilities by effectively using your calendar. Place your most important work in your Outlook calendar and use the alerts so that you don't forget. Review your calendar each week and each day. This will help you retain control and keep you from feeling overwhelmed.

As you schedule your tasks, always leave time for personal care. Dedicated professionals typically make clients and work the primary focus of life. That's good to a point. But when we neglect ourselves, we eventually become overwhelmed and increasingly disorganized. So if you set a time to go to the gym or to the doctor or on a vacation, don't allow new requests and ongoing obligations to upend your plans.

You can overcome procrastination! By developing a plan and practicing what I've outlined in this chapter, you will find more time to focus on the work you really enjoy, and gain freedom from the incessant negativity of your inner critic. Identify one or two tips from this chapter that feel right for you and give them a try for a month. If you have success, then try another tip.

CHAPTER 3

AVOID MULTITASKING

ELECTRONIC POP-UPS, impromptu office drop-ins, email pings, voice mails, worry, concern, stress, frustration, urgent requests, doorbells . . . these are just some of the many distractions that can interrupt our concentration at work and at home. They prevent us from being focused on strategic work. In fact, a study funded by Hewlett-Packard and conducted by the Institute of Psychiatry found that "workers distracted by email and phone calls suffered from an IQ reduction of more than twice that found in marijuana smokers." For every distraction it can take twenty-five minutes to regain focus. That reduction in productivity affects the bottom line of our businesses and increases the hours we have to spend at work to complete projects.

A typical approach to handling distractions is to "multitask." We think we are good at doing multiple tasks at the same time, but it doesn't work. In my OWNyourTIME® workshops, I always ask the participants to raise their hands if they think they are good at multitasking. Nearly everyone does. Then I ask how many of them have made mistakes while multitasking. Invariably, the same hands go up. The fact is, we perceive ourselves as being good at multitasking, but in reality our brains cannot do multiple things at once very well. Research has concluded that the brain is designed to focus on one task at a time.

I had an embarrassing situation a number of years ago when working in business development for a Fortune 500 company. I was on a conference call and sending emails to a prospective client at the same time. The conversation didn't seem relevant to me at that time and I didn't think that my participation would be important until later in the call. I *thought* I was listening and paying attention to the call, so I decided to maximize my time and also send out an email to my prospective client.

Unexpectedly, someone on the call asked me a question. I was caught off-guard. I had no idea what they were talking about. I was completely unprepared to answer the question. To add insult to injury, I ended up addressing my email to the wrong person! I picked up one of the names that was mentioned on the call and used that as my email greeting to my prospective client. That was embarrassing! Because I was not paying attention to the conference call or the email, I messed up on both and had to do a lot of work to make up for my mistake. It took me three times longer to recover from all this than if I had just focused on one task at a time.

The more we split our attention among various responsibilities, the less efficient we become. A research study conducted in 2010 by neuroscientists at the French medical research agency, INSERM, concluded that when people try to focus on two tasks at the same time, each side of the brain tackles a different task. For example, if you are driving and texting, the primary part of your brain may be focused on texting while the secondary part of your brain is focused on driving. You are not completely focused on either task.

In a Stanford University study published in *Inc.* magazine, Clifford Nass asked 262 Stanford students to complete experiments that involved focusing on one task at a time versus multitasking. In every test, students who spent less time multitasking on their electronic devices performed the best.

In order to prevent distractions from hijacking our

concentration we need tools and a plan that can help us stay on task. Nass suggested what he calls the twenty-minute rule. Rather than switching tasks from minute to minute, dedicate a twenty-minute chunk of time to a single task, then switch to the next one.

There are many ways to combat the multitasking habit. The first way is self-awareness, to be cognizant of when you are multitasking and to recognize that it leads to lower productivity. Another strategy is to minimize your desire to multitask by focusing on the outcome you want to achieve. Tell yourself: I want to focus on my work so that I don't make mistakes and have to spend ten times as long correcting my work. I want to avoid looking at my phone while driving so that I can get home safely. You get the idea. Understanding that your actions always have consequences will help you limit multitasking and stay focused on one thing at a time.

CHAPTER 4

SAY NO AND SAVE TIME

TIME MANAGEMENT TAKES DISCIPLINE, self-control, and practice. The odds of getting it right the first time are against you, and you'll likely fail several times in your attempt to master it. But good habits don't often come easy. If time-management habits were automatic, everyone would be as productive as you will become.

A key to managing your time is to learn to say no to the plethora of requests and demands that invade your daily work schedule and personal time. The problem is that business professionals and company leaders often think they shouldn't ever say no to anything, for reasons we'll talk about in this chapter. But to maximize your time, you need to say no to distractions, no to multitasking, no to answering emails all day long.

Some of the most common distractions come from the Internet, cell phones, text messages, email, and highly social colleagues. Once you are able to recognize which distractions are wasting your time, then you can set boundaries and restrictions that will help you regain ownership of your time.

WORK OFF-LINE

While writing this chapter, I forgot to turn off my Outlook pop-ups. Every time I got one, I would look to see who it was from. I saw that there was a shoe sale and soon I was shopping online. As a result of this distraction, it took me forty minutes longer to finish writing this chapter. So when you need to focus, turn off the pop-ups and push your notifications.

There is no better way to eliminate computer distractions than to remove the biggest one of all—the Internet. Turn off your Wi-Fi for forty minutes and you will immediately gain control of your time.

STIFLE YOUR CELL PHONE

Your cell phone is an amazing tool. It's also an amazing distraction! Sometimes you have to say no to the cell phone. Did you know you can set your phone to "Do Not Disturb" mode and only allow specific phone numbers to ring? Use this as a way of temporarily blocking calls while still allowing calls from people who might need you in an emergency.

SHUT THE DOOR!

If you have off-the-charts charisma (I'm sure you do), your office is probably a natural meeting place for your colleagues. This is evidence that the social side of your work is going very well. All that friendly attention during the day, however, will require you to work long hours at night and on weekends. And that will upset your social life outside the office.

It's great to be popular, but sometimes you have to say no to office visits. How do you do this without losing your popularity? To manage the traffic heading into your office, I suggest closing your door when you need to concentrate. This is not rude; it's an efficient communication tool. When we leave office doors open, we train our colleagues (or family, if you work from home) to pop in whenever they want.

Think of it this way. If each office chat results in twenty-five minutes of lost productivity and you have at least two drop-ins per day, then you are likely losing fifty minutes of daily productivity. Now that you know how much time each distraction will cost you, ask yourself if you want all those social visits.

I understand that organizations want everyone to be approachable in the workplace; however, if you are able to manage the flow of visitors that come your way, you will be recognized as someone who gets work done, and that will telegraph to others that they need to follow your lead.

Moreover, you can begin to retrain people to respect the closed door and then schedule a time to meet you when you are free. When you don't need to concentrate intently, then you can keep your door open.

You need to use good judgment, of course. I recommend allowing your boss into your office anytime. Inform her that you keep your door closed so as to stay focused on work, but that she is always welcome.

If the closed door approach to saying no needs reinforcement, I also recommend removing comfortable chairs from your office so that your colleagues don't feel so inclined to use your office as a lounge. If you want to keep your chairs, you can load them up with books and files so no one can sit down.

NOISE SUPPRESSION

If you work in an office with an open floor plan, it's a good idea to wear noise canceling headphones. This is a way to close the door of an office when there are no doors. You don't even have to play music. Wearing the headphones sends a gentle message that you don't wish to be disturbed. Colleagues will understand that it's not a good time for socializing when you are wearing headphones.

If you are able to say no to distractions, you will be recognized as someone who gets things done. It's likely that others will follow your example and become equally productive.

CHAPTER 5

PAVLOV'S PING

WE CANNOT LEAVE OUR EMAILS ALONE. Or is it that our emails won't leave us alone? Whatever the case, with the advent of smartphones we check email every time we hear the ever-present ping. In fact, many people check emails at the dinner table, in bed before they go to sleep, and as soon as they wake up.

Research shows that when we get interrupted by an email ping our bodies release a chemical called dopamine, which has been around since prehistoric times. It's a neurotransmitter released by certain types of neurons in the brain when we experience pleasure. Perhaps because humans find great joy in being socially connected, dopamine can be released when we hear a cellphone ping. That sound represents relational connections. Someone wants or needs us! That, in turn, can produce a strong urge to check our phones every time we hear the alert.

This is similar to Pavlov's experiment. During the

1890s, Russian physiologist Ivan Pavlov found an unconditioned response in dogs by showing them a bowl of food and measuring how much saliva they produced. He then conducted experiments by feeding his dogs and ringing a bell. In the next step of the experiment, he would ring the bell but offer the dogs no food. The dogs would salivate upon hearing the bell ring, even if there was no food.

It seems that, like Pavlov's dogs, we have become conditioned to respond to the sounds of our electronic devices. As a result, it is common for people to check email frequently from the time they wake up until they go to bed late at night.

You might think this is a minor issue. It's not. I worked with an executive who asked me to help her with stress. She was feeling anxious all the time and was only sleeping four hours a night. In fact, her stress was so bad it caused her to have a panic attack that landed her in the hospital! Upon reviewing her work schedule, I discovered that she was checking and responding to emails until 2 a.m. She had good reason to check her emails at that hour because many of her clients were in Asia. But she did not make up for lost sleep by waking up later. She still woke up at 5:30 a.m.

How to Avoid Being a Pavlov Dog

I recently read an article that said most people check email fifty-six times a day. Ideally you should only check your email every two hours. It can be hard to break your habit; two hours without checking might cause jitters. So start slow. Instead of checking email every six minutes, try to check it every twenty minutes. I encourage you to set a timer for twenty-minute increments. Then you can decide if you want to bump it up to every thirty minutes or every hour. See how you do.

Some people believe that they need to constantly check email in order to be available and responsive to their team and clients. Immediate responsiveness is the norm for professionals today. But instantly answering every request can distract you from important tasks and reduce your productivity, and that will have a detrimental impact on your team.

One way to circumvent this challenge is to use the "out-of-office" notification in your email service. Here is an example of an out-of-office notification that I use when I'm focusing on a project: "I will be in a meeting between 11 a.m. and 1 p.m. today. If this email is urgent and requires immediate attention, please call me or contact my assistant. Otherwise, I will get back to you by 2 p.m." By using an out-of-office message, you can take control of your time and complete tasks without distractions. Give it a try.

SETTING BOUNDARIES

In addition to reducing the frequency of email checks, we can also set cut-off times for when we read email and when we don't. Schedule the start and ending times for when you will check and respond to email. It takes discipline, but refuse to check email before and after the cut-off times you establish.

Your boundaries might depend on your job's working hours, but a non-negotiable boundary for me is to stop checking email after 8:30 p.m. The reason is simple. If I receive an email at night that causes me distress, the result is a restless night of sleep followed by next-day fatigue. In most cases, you cannot solve a work problem after business hours, so the end result is just added stress and reduced productivity.

Whenever you set your end-of-day boundary, check your email one last time and then set your phone to "Do Not Disturb," or simply turn it off. Get a great night's sleep, refresh your batteries, and start again in the morning.

How to Manage Your Inbox

Research conducted by The Radicati Group calculated the number of emails typical business professionals send and receive on a daily basis. The number was astounding: about 189 emails per day. Handling this amount of information can be overwhelming.

Time-management coaches differ greatly on their approaches to managing an email inbox. Some recommend a net-zero approach, which means that by the end of each day you have checked your emails, responded, and filed or deleted all of them. The next day you start anew with zero emails from the previous day in your inbox. If you can be that dedicated to your inbox, and if you get stressed when your inbox isn't empty at the end of the day, then this might be a great method for you. For most of my clients, however, this approach is too time consuming. As soon as their emails are at net-zero, they get a new email that messes things up again. It feels to them like the Greek myth of Sisyphus, who was condemned for eternity to roll a rock up a mountain only to have it roll down every time he reached the top.

I have heard the concerns of many business professionals who struggle to manage their inbox. Some have a good handle on email management while others might have over sixty thousand emails from the past five years lurking in their inbox. This clutter causes anxiety. People feel overwhelmed and out of control.

If you find yourself in this situation, rest assured that there is a way out of the email mess. There are strategies you can implement right now to manage your inbox more effectively. Here are the three steps I recommend.

Step 1: Set a timer. Do this every time you go into your email account, especially first thing in the morning. I recommend setting the timer for fifteen minutes. This is the time you will use to handle email at various times during each day. Use this fifteen-minute block of email management time every two or three hours (as I described earlier). I usually use the timer on my phone; however, there are some great apps, such as InFocus and Pomodoro Time.

Step 2: Delete, unsubscribe, file. After you've set your timer, go through your email one by one. Delete emails that are irrelevant and unneeded. When you come across a blog post that you'll never read, delete it and unsubscribe. If you need information on a topic in the blog, just do an Internet search at a later time.

You will probably notice that you have been cc'd on emails for whom another person is the primary recipient. This can add a lot of clutter to an inbox. Many times people include us in email threads about issues that don't pertain to us. They send them for politeness or record keeping. If you don't need an email of this type, just delete it. If you think it's important, file it immediately. This way you will be able to reference it later without allowing it to interfere with your agenda.

Step 3: Respond. As you go through your emails in that fifteen-minute block of time, you will respond to all of them. First deal with those emails that require a quick answer and not much thought. Then, for emails that require significant attention, I suggest that you inform the sender that you will reply by a certain time. Put a note in Outlook or in your calendar that sets aside time to respond to the email. Be sure to fulfill your promise! This is an effective method because it shows the other person that you are attending to their needs while not allowing email to dominate life.

There are times when email from a major client or boss must be answered fully and immediately. Good judgment is important, of course. But in most cases, people just want assurance that you have received the email request and that you will be sending a response.

The most important thing is to stay in control of your time. When we drop what we are doing to respond to the constant email drip, we give up ownership of our time and hand it over to someone else. As long as you stick to the ideas in this chapter you will control your time and still communicate well with your colleagues and clients.

CHAPTER 6

THINK STRATEGICALLY EVERY DAY

LET'S IMAGINE THAT YOU GET ON A PLANE, place your carry-on bags in the upper bin, and settle into your seat. All of sudden the pilot says: "Ladies and gentlemen, welcome to flight 401. I have not had time to develop a flight plan for this trip, but we're in a terrible hurry; so we're just going to take off and figure it out as we go." Would you stay on that airplane?

This is the way many of us live and work. We have no flight plan. We are so busy with managing the details of life that we never stop to think strategically about our businesses, professional direction, or personal lives. We just "figure it out as we go."

The problems with this approach to life are obvious (I'll state them anyway). Without strategic thinking, without a "flight plan," you start to feel anxious and lost. You aren't really sure where you are going. Without a clear destination in mind, you will get to the end of the year and not know if you made any progress.

You'll feel tired and burned out because after all your hard work you won't feel like you have anything tangible to show for it.

Many books have been written about developing "habits for success," or figuring out your life's mission statement, or identifying your deepest values. These books can help, but they have a critical shortfall: Even as you read about habits and values, and even as you write your mission statement, your phone is ringing, your text messages are pinging, your email account is flooding, your kids are begging for attention, and your next deadline is breathing down your neck. Then your spouse is frustrated because you're always working. In other words, all the best efforts to develop habits and live according to our values are pointless—if we don't learn how to manage our time.

My approach is different. We have to plan time for strategic thinking *every day*. Isn't that what pilots do? At every stopover, you see them sitting in the cockpit mapping out the next flight plan. Strategic planning is part of a pilot's daily routine. They recognize that the best way to protect time for strategic thinking is to make it a daily task! Likewise, we need to make sure that we set aside daily time to think about new and long-range opportunities, business trends, or product innovation as part of our daily task list.

Tony Blair, former prime minister of the United Kingdom, in an interview at Stanford University, said that when he first came into office President Bill Clinton offered him some advice. Blair thought Clinton might offer tips about how to create world peace or solve global economic problems. But Clinton said one word: "scheduling." Clinton said that scheduling was crucial "because if you don't manage your schedule and make time every day to think about the big picture, then the system will take over and you won't accomplish anything in office."

To include strategic thinking in a daily schedule, I recommend that you write down three key objectives that you would like to accomplish. These objectives can be part of a bigger strategy or they can be stand-alone plans. They can be very broad, such as planning the next year's budget priorities, or studying market trends, or evaluating the needs of your key leaders. The point is to think about the big picture.

Some people get stressed about thinking strategically. Trying to develop big plans and long-term visions can seem overwhelming. So as you think strategically each day, I recommend that you break up long-range plans into smaller components. Dividing big plans into smaller parts can prevent us from being paralyzed by the immensity of a large vision. We can also overcome procrastination when we have a clear starting point and clear steps toward the overall goal.

Instead of living under the control of little fires and busy work, remember to think strategically every day. You will be amazed to see your progress and achievements when you look back and review the year.

CHAPTER 7

MAKING ACCURATE TIME ESTIMATES

GOOD TIME MANAGEMENT is about more than fending off distractions. It's also about making accurate estimates of the time it will take to complete tasks. Do you really know how long it will take you to perform a job? Are you able to quantify how long you are able to concentrate so that you can complete the work?

We frequently underestimate how long something will take us to finish. If a client asks you to deliver a proposal by the end of the day and you think it will only take twenty minutes, your assumption is usually wrong. That's because distractions, short attention-spans and poor concentration can turn a twenty-minute task into a one-hour ordeal. Underestimating the time required for your work can result in working late, missed deadlines, and stress. Therefore, it is crucial to understand the connections between time estimation, attention spans, and distractions.

There is a difference between attention spans and

the ability to concentrate. When we talk about attention spans, we are referring to how long people typically watch a TV show before flipping to the next station. Advertisers study this and know that commercials need to be fast-paced and not more than thirty seconds long. Measuring attention spans is about studying how long we stay interested in something. This not the same as how long we can sustain concentration.

In 2015, Microsoft published a study on attention spans. The findings were surprising. They concluded that typical adults have an attention span of roughly eight seconds. That is down from the previously recorded twelve seconds. The study found that this reduction is a direct result of digital distractions.

Microsoft also concluded that our typical attention span is shorter than that of goldfish, which have nine-second attention spans. So there you have it: Goldfish have longer attention spans that most people.

Remember that attention spans are different than concentration abilities. To get an idea of how long you can concentrate, some research suggests adding one year to your age and then converting that number into minutes. That number will be the amount of time (in minutes) that you should be able to sustain concentrated work. In other words, if you are thirty-years old you should be able to sustain concentrated, focused work for thirty-one minutes. (At some point in old age, attention spans decrease.)

Other research suggests that regardless of one's age, most people can't concentrate for more than twenty-five minutes at a time. For me it's around twenty to twenty-five minutes, if uninterrupted. I use this knowledge about myself when I am planning my day so that I can block off about twenty-five minutes for work that has to be done without interruption.

ESTIMATING YOUR CONCENTRATION TIME

The best way to figure out how much time to reserve for a task is to understand your own concentration and work patterns. Here is a simple way to do that.

Make a table with three vertical columns and multiple horizontal rows. Label the first column "Tasks," the second column "Estimated Time," and the third column "Actual Time."

Next, write a sampling of your tasks in the horizontal rows under the "tasks" column. Write down the time you think it will take for each task in the "estimated time" column. Finally, after you have finished the tasks, write down how long they actually took to finish in the third column.

Be sure to time yourself so that you can see if your estimates are true to reality. The more frequently you do this exercise, the better you will be able to estimate the amount of time it will actually take to do your work.

If you don't like making charts, you can also set a timer for twenty or twenty-five minutes and see if you can finish the amount of work you thought you could complete in that time or not. Do this simple test often and your improved self-awareness will enable you to make more accurate time estimates.

I had a client who did this exercise and it helped immensely. She is an engineer who works in the mining industry, and she has many reports to analyze and research each day. Due to her heavy workload, she found herself working into the wee hours of the night. This became a vicious cycle of fatigue and stress. After doing the exercise, she realized that she wasn't allowing enough time to complete her work.

In response, she bumped up the amount of time she would need for certain activities to forty-five minutes. She reported to me that she was able to get more done in that uninterrupted block of time than she ever had before. In fact, she sent me a note saying that she now felt like a good mother because she wasn't so distracted by her obligations when she was home; she was now getting her work done—at the office.

Remember that the more self-awareness you have of your daily concentration and attention-span patterns the better you will be at making accurate time estimates. This will reduce stress and balance your life.

CHAPTER 8

BRAIN DUMPING

FOCUSING ON WORK CAN BE DIFFICULT or impossible when you have too much on your mind. You start the day knowing what you need to do and you are highly motivated to finish the work. But then you can't filter, categorize, or prioritize all the thoughts in your busy mind. Your best intentions are left unfulfilled.

The other challenge happens when you try to remember the important and not-so-important thoughts in your head. Sometimes, when I am presenting in front of an audience, I will suddenly remember that I have to do something mundane, like buy a birthday card or dish soap. This will distract me right at the moment I need to speak. And what's also frustrating is that I almost immediately forget what I needed by the time I get home. I'll think of something that distracts me, and then I forget about it five minutes later.

All the clutter in my mind disrupts my productivity. Left unmanaged, it just sits there waiting for inopportune times to distract me from important work. All it takes is for someone to say something that reminded me of another task and I become totally distracted from what I was working on. These triggers can help us remember important ideas, but they have to be managed so that we can stay focused and productive.

To avoid the constant interruptions of a busy mind and the stress caused by not wanting to forget important things, I suggest "brain dumping." It works like this: First, carry a notebook (paper, not digital) and use it to jot down thoughts or tasks the moment they pop into your mind. I suggest buying a funky notebook, one so wild looking that it won't get lost on your desk. I worked with an attorney who is a tough-as-nails litigator. He bought a bright green notebook with daisies on it. All his random thoughts, ideas, and tasks would be dumped into that notebook, which allowed him to stay focused on the work of the moment.

This technique is better than placing sticky notes on your walls and computers. (I once walked into a busy office and saw the receptionist had two of these notes stuck to her chest. I guess that might work, but it's not the best fashion statement.) You could use the voice recorder on your smart phone, but I recommend a paper notebook. Based on my experience, dictating thoughts into phones is more cumbersome than jotting them down in my notebook. Finding your thoughts in an audio recording is time-consuming. But if you still want to use your smart phone, take a picture of your notes rather than recording audio. If you want to use your phone to take notes, keep in mind that phones can be a distraction; that's why I recommend going "old school." Not everyone has the willpower to jot down notes into a phone without checking texts and emails at the same time. If you do have the willpower, then take advantage of the technology. If not, use paper.

Once you have your random thoughts "dumped" in a notebook, a good next step is to categorize them at the end of the day or first thing in the morning. Prioritize them from most important to least important so you can tackle them in the right order.

Brain dumping will free your mind to focus on bigger projects. The key to successful brain dumping is to always keep your notebook with you and use it when a thought like "I need to buy toothpaste" pops into your head.

CHAPTER 9

ENERGY, REST, AND PRODUCTIVITY

AFTER A DAY OF COACHING MEETINGS, I had to pick up my son from high school. While waiting for him in the parking lot, I could feel my eyes start to droop and my breathing become deeper. Ten minutes later my son was knocking on the car window. I had the horrific realization that I had fallen asleep with my mouth wide open, as if catching flies, while a parking lot full of teenagers gawked. Despite my embarrassment, there was a silver lining: I realized that I felt better and had enough energy to carry on with my afternoon.

What does time management have to do with energy? If you feel tired, overwhelmed, and out of fuel, you know how much longer it takes to finish your work. But we lead such busy lives that it's difficult to get enough rest. Some of my clients work from early in the morning to late at night without taking restful breaks. As a result, productivity lags.

Tony Schwartz, founder of the Energy Project and

author of many articles on time and energy management for *Harvard Business Review,* has conducted extensive research on how to be more productive by including better rest into our routines. Although we all have the same 1440 minutes in a day, his research showed that we do have control over how much energy we expend in a day. Schwartz found that continuous renewals of energy help us become more productive.

By understanding how energy and rest is related to improved well-being and productivity we can manage life better and be less stressed.

Managing Your Energy Peaks and Valleys

Over fifty years ago, sleep researcher Nathaniel Kleitman discovered the "rest-activity cycle." This is a ninety-minute sleep period in which we move through five stages of sleep. Kleitman also observed that our bodies operate with the same ninety-minute cycles during the day; we move from higher to lower states of alertness in ninety-minute cycles.

We all are aware of these daily energy peaks and valleys. They are called ultradium cycles. When we start to have that lackluster feeling, we often head to the coffee maker, or we grab a handful of chocolates from the colleague who keeps a bowl of them on her desk. Chocolate grazing usually happens during the latter part of the ultradium cycle. A less caloric and more effective way to manage low energy is to take a break, stand up, walk around, or meditate for five minutes.

You might think that meditation would cause you to become even more sleepy, but meditating will increase your focus and energy. You can do it at your desk without ever getting caught. Just turn your chair so it faces away from the door and set a timer for five-to-ten minutes. Then sit still with your feet on the floor and your eyes closed. Hold a book or document in your hand as a prop, just in case someone peeks into your office. Then begin the process of meditation. There are some great apps that provide guided meditation. One that I am fond of is called Simply Being. Another way to meditate is to count your breaths with a five-second inhale and a five-second exhale.

When we meditate we reduce levels of cortisol, the hormone that our bodies generate when we are stressed, overwhelmed, and over-worked. Without a way to reduce the cortisol levels in our bodies, we can more easily go into a fight-or-flight response. This response was documented by McGill University alum

Hans Selve, in 1936. He concluded that when we are under stress, cortisol is released into our system causing us to have a strong need to take action. A physical release is needed to reduce cortisol levels. This is very difficult to do in today's workplace because we are usually sitting at a desk or in endless meetings. When there is no physical release, cortisol levels build up in our blood. This has a negative effect on mind and body.

The fight-or-flight response worked well when we were hunters and gatherers. We needed it to protect ourselves and our tribes. But in today's world, this response has no outlet. It actually reduces our ability to solve problems and think clearly. For this reason, understanding the importance of reducing cortisol is critical to improved happiness, decreased stress, and increased productivity.

When you relax, the right side of your brain (the creative side) will become more active. By meditating, even for a short period, another neurotransmitter called serotonin is released. Serotonin, unlike cortisol, is released when you are in a calm state. When there is more serotonin in your blood, your fight-or-flight response is not activated and you are better able to solve problems and develop creative ideas. Have you ever noticed when the most brilliant ideas come to your mind? For me it's in the shower or while I'm driving to work—not when I am stressed out at my desk.

There are other ways to reduce stress. In addition to meditation, exercise provides an amazing cortisol release. Listening intently to music and adding more laughter and humor into your life are also great ways to reduce stress. My family, if you asked them, would tell you that I am an incredibly serious person. It's hard for me to be light-hearted, so I actively seek it out. A few years ago, I joined an improvisational group and was forced to be silly and playful. I still smile when I reflect on that fun experience. I encourage you to pursue activities that make you laugh. Doing so will help you reduce stress and increase serotonin.

At the office, you can walk during breaks and get away from your desk at lunch. It helps to sit with colleagues or go out. You can also catch small breaks in your day with one-minute breathing routines.

Another and perhaps more controversial way to re-energize is by taking a quick nap. Research shows that performance at work increases after a brief *siesta*. Google has nap rooms. If one of the largest companies in the world can have nap rooms, maybe your company could invest in a few, too. Don't laugh, it could happen.

There is also that radical idea of getting a good night's sleep. It's clear that plenty of sleep leads to higher productivity, better ability to solve problems, improved creativity, and even increased revenue. A good night's rest might generate a breakthrough idea on a new product. Or perhaps you will feel more confident about marketing your services. You've heard the cliché "time is money." Well, maybe we should say "sleep is money."

ULTRADIUM CYCLES AND WORK SCHEDULES

During the workday, we face different types of work. Some work requires high levels of energy, thought, and creativity. Other work can almost be done on auto-pilot. It's helpful if we can align the type of work we do with our ultradium cycles.

I suggest that my clients pay attention to when they are typically at a peak energy level and when they are at a low energy level during each day. Having recognized these individual patterns, they can build a work schedule that is in harmony with the natural cycle.

I am a morning person. I think well and am very focused between the hours of 8 a.m. and noon. I've learned that mornings are a great time for me to see clients. Likewise, I try to avoid late afternoon coaching sessions because I am not at my energetic peak.

These cycles can also apply to a weekly schedule. A few years ago, while I was working as a corporate salesperson, my employer asked me to make sales calls on Monday mornings. Although I had great energy in the morning, making calls at the start of the week was a hard pill for me to swallow. I hated the idea and had no positive energy for it. Don't tell my former boss this, but I simply didn't make those calls on Monday mornings. I found that Friday afternoons were a better time to make calls because I was more optimistic.

If you find that you're spending your mornings doing work that would be better accomplished in the afternoon, consider switching your projects around. If you align your work with your energy levels, you will better serve your clients and you'll be more productive.

CHAPTER 10

MEETING MADNESS!

THE NUMBER ONE DISTRACTION identified by organizations is too many meetings. Executive leaders, managers, and employees all say they are not able to finish their work in a timely manner or think creatively because of excessive meetings.

Companies obviously need to schedule meetings in order to get everyone on the same page and to make conclusive decisions, but there should be a limit on the number of meetings allowed per person.

I had a client who was an executive at a publicly traded Fortune 500 company. He kept telling me that he didn't know where his time was going. A time audit revealed that he spent roughly fifty-five hours a month in meetings. That is more than one work-week of meetings every month! No wonder he was stressed, aggravated, and frustrated.

As his coach, I helped him categorize each meeting. There were investment meetings, HR meetings, sales meetings, board meetings, marketing and PR meetings. Then I asked him how much time was needed to prepare for each meeting and how much time he typically needed to allocate to tasks following the meetings. We put a number of minutes or hours next to each one on the list. We then identified which meetings were mandatory for him to attend and which ones he could skip or delegate to a colleague who could take notes for him. At the end of this exercise, we were able to eliminate about twenty-five hours of meetings a month from his calendar. I could see the relief in his eyes when he realized he was getting his time back.

All too often we accept meeting invitations without asking why we were invited or if we need to attend. We almost always accept these invitations because we don't want to insult our colleagues, and because we want to be good team players.

How can we limit the number of meetings we attend and still maintain a good reputation? There are many ways to manage this. You can say no and then develop a meeting attendance plan. Here are some proven ideas.

First, when possible, delegate your participation to someone else, such as an assistant. Ask the person to take notes and send them after the meeting. This way you will know what took place at the meeting and you can contribute feedback if necessary. This shows that you respect the intent of the meeting and the person requesting your time.

Second, make sure there is an agenda for every meeting you attend. Prior to the meeting, ask the person responsible for running it to set one. Without an agenda, meetings can run long and drift away from the meeting's purpose.

Third, if you are responsible for running a meeting, verify that you have thought carefully about the important questions below.

Do all the people you plan to invite need to attend? If for some the answer is no, then remove those names from the list. Believe me, they will appreciate it.

Can you keep the meeting to less than thirty minutes? Research shows that meetings shorter than thirty minutes are much more productive, efficient, and better attended than those scheduled for sixty minutes.

Do I have an agenda typed and printed for this meeting? Many think they can run meetings by memory, but that's rarely true. When sending out the agenda, make sure to give all attendees sufficient time to look it over and prepare. This could be a few days or a few weeks prior to the meeting, depending on how much has to get done and how frequently you meet. Allow specific amounts of time in the agenda for each topic and speaker. To keep the meeting on time, use a timer.

Who is facilitating? Every meeting needs a facilitator; otherwise, one person can take over the conversation and nothing will be accomplished. Make sure to identify who will facilitate before the meeting starts.

Does this meeting have a clear purpose? If the answer is no, then spend some time to clarify your objectives and list the desired outcomes. You'd be surprised to know how many meetings are held without a clear purpose.

Will this meeting outline clear action items? It's important that each person understands the follow-up action items for which they are responsible.

Can we have a no-smartphone zone? A huge distraction, and an area of frustration for me, is when everyone is looking at phones during a meeting. So, at the start of every meeting, I ask attendees to put their phones away unless they are waiting for some life-changing news. I had a client who asked all attendees to put their names on Post-it Notes, stick the notes on their phones, and leave the phones in a basket before the meeting.

By reviewing these questions at the beginning of each week, you can lead meetings that are shorter and more productive. I encourage you to refer back to these suggestions regularly.

Here's to fewer meetings!

CHAPTER 11

PERFECTION PARALYSIS

Striving to be perfect has its good side, but let's be honest: Perfectionism can paralyze us and zap productivity. It often leads to missed opportunities, blown deadlines, massive stress, and frustration with ourselves and others. If we can learn to tame the voice in our head that says, "It's still not good enough," then we can free our minds and schedules to conquer other important initiatives.

I had a client who was a student at the University of Colorado. She came to me because she was having a horrible struggle to turn in her school assignments on time. This inability to complete her work by her professors' deadlines led her to feel frustrated and angry with herself. Her self-confidence and grades dropped.

Shortly after we began working on time-management strategies together, I began to notice a pattern with her. Whenever she received a new assignment, she would begin researching in earnest but never start writing. When I asked her why she spent so much time on research and so little time completing the work, she said that she never felt the research was done. In fact, she was over-prepared. She just never thought her work was perfect. This tendency sabotaged her ability to finish written assignments on time. She was more willing to accept a lower grade due to a missed deadline than to turn in "imperfect" work. I call her problem Perfection Paralysis.

If you deal with poor productivity, then you might be suffering from Perfection Paralysis as well. Although you won't find this syndrome in the official book of psychological disorders, this is a real problem that's not easy to overcome—unless you are perfect.

In the case of my client (let's call her Holly), we tackled the problem by dividing a whiteboard into three sections. In one section, we wrote all the things that could happen if she handed in an assignment as "good enough." In the middle section, we made a list of what a "perfect" assignment would look like. Then, in the third section, we made a list of consequences for not handing in the assignment at all.

After reviewing the list, Holly realized that she couldn't describe what perfection would look like. She discovered that perfection is an elusive ideal. Thus her pursuit of perfection was a constant exercise in frustration and disappointment.

Avoiding the trap of perfectionism doesn't mean that you should do lousy work or be content with subpar performance. Holly's example simply highlights how we can sabotage ourselves and our time when we seek perfection without actually knowing what that means. Even if we could come up with a perfect definition of "perfect," few are able to attain it. Think about it: The best baseball players in the world have batting averages of only about .300!

Later on, I received a text from Holly. "I can't believe it!" she said. "I got all of my assignments in on time and graduated with a GPA of 3.65." From almost not being able to graduate on time to graduating on time with a high GPA was a huge accomplishment. The Perfection Paralysis lesson will help her throughout her career.

PERFECTIONIST LEADERS

Perfectionism also affects business leaders, and that can affect the entire team they lead. If you are in a position of company leadership, and if you think you might be a perfectionist, it's important to be cautious about the impact of this trait on your team. If you expect "perfection" from others, you will likely make it hard for your team to complete projects in a timely manner. You delegate work. You are never satisfied with the team's efforts. The team becomes paralyzed. That's what happens.

As we saw earlier, perfection is hard to define, even for ourselves. Therefore, perfectionist leaders typically fail to communicate their expectations of perfection to others. As a result, leaders are perpetually disappointed with the team's work, which in turn frustrates the team, reduces morale, and complicates relationships.

Many years ago, I had a boss who fit this category. I was working with a graphic artist on packaging designs. Once the design was completed, my boss (who was not a graphic designer) would take out a ruler and measure every inch of the package to compare it to other versions. There was no reason to do this. Measuring packaging designs was a waste of time and money. He sought some form of perfection that he was unable to define or communicate to others. As a result, we were striving to achieve something intangible, and that wasted time and increased stress.

Test Your Perfectionism Level

Here's a short test you can take to evaluate your level of perfectionism. Answer yes or no to each question and then tally your score at the end.

1. I prefer to work alone because only I can do it right.

2. People often say my expectations are unrealistic.

3. Making decisions is difficult because I fear mistakes.

4. I get stressed when people don't do things my way.

5. I tie my self-confidence to how others perceive me.

6. I focus on my mistakes and rarely on my successes.

7. I often miss deadlines to make improvements.

8. I often fall short of my own expectations.

9. All my work is very important; it's hard to prioritize.

10. I often work through the night.

11. I worry excessively.

12. I seem to cause stress within my teams.

Now add up the number of times you answered yes and use the scoring system below to help you figure out how much perfectionism affects your life.

1-3: You have some perfectionist qualities, which may hold you back slightly.

4-6: You have moderate perfectionist traits that cause you to miss some deadlines and experience more stress. Pay attention because these characteristics might be holding you back from achieving greater success.

7-12: You have a strong perfectionist tendency. It's time to take a hard look at where you are in your career and how your colleagues perceive you. Perfectionism might be having a very negative impact on your life.

Tips for Overcoming Perfection Paralysis

Awareness is the key to overcoming detrimental behavior. Once you recognize an obstacle, then you can manage it and have others hold you accountable for the changes you want to make. Taking small steps with the tips listed below will reduce self-inflicted stress, boost productivity, and increase the satisfaction you get from completing a project on time.

1. Use the whiteboard exercise I used with Holly.

2. Do your best, finish the job, deliver on time.

3. Learn to delegate; allow your team to work their way.

4. If you have a perfectionist tendency, keep it in check.

5. Aim for a quality product not a perfect product.

Remember that perfection is hard to define and almost impossible to attain. Do your best to produce high quality work and then . . . relax.

CHAPTER 12

PRIORITIZATION

WE ALL HAVE A MILLION THINGS TO DO and they all seem urgent. So how do we gain control over the chaos? It's not going to happen by putting sticky notes on your computer screen, windshield, or all over your fridge. Prioritization takes thought—and a strategy.

I have two ways to go about prioritizing your work and your life. The first is for business leaders who are responsible for generating company revenue. The second is for all other professionals.

PRIORITIES FOR GENERATING REVENUE

If you are responsible for sales and revenue to grow a business—that is, if you are in the business of eating what you kill—then you need to prioritize your work according to that crucial goal. Start by making a list of all your tasks each week. New demands will pop up unexpectedly (there are always grass fires to put out). But making a list of all the work you know you will need to do during the week is the best way to set priorities.

The next step is to review your list and identify which activities will help you produce revenue. For example, by writing a new client proposal and submitting it, I place myself in a position to sell a new program. That, in turn, will generate revenue for my company. By contrast, doing expense reports will reimburse my business but it will not generate revenue.

Once you've identified your revenue activities, focus all your attention on those tasks first. I suggest starting with the work that most excites you. Make sure that you focus on these tasks at a time of day when you have a lot of energy. Deploy your amazing charisma and creativity when they are at full force.

The flip side of that coin is to do "administrative" tasks when you are not full of vim and vigor. No matter how tempted you are to check your email inbox, don't squander your best moments on tasks that won't yield revenue. Save all the busy work for the times of day when you have the least energy.

The rest of this chapter applies to all professionals, and it has everything to do with President Eisenhower.

PRIORITIZATION FOR EVERYONE

All professionals need to set good priorities to improve productivity. One of the best and easiest ways to do this is with the prioritization model developed by President Dwight Eisenhower.

Before becoming president, Eisenhower was a five-star Army general. He served two terms as president with his last ending in 1961. His programs led to the development of the interstate highway system, NASA, and the basic workings of the Internet.

Eisenhower was recognized as a master of time management. He was extremely efficient and productive. He used to say, "If everything is an emergency, then nothing is an emergency." He also said, "What is important is seldom urgent." Eisenhower was able to distinguish urgency from importance. He recognized that these two categories were the keys to managing time well. We can define what's "urgent" and "important" using the following definitions.

Urgent tasks demand your immediate attention. These tasks might include responding to your board of directors, getting your health insurance filed before the enrollment period ends, submitting your taxes on time, or picking up kids from school.

Important tasks will help you achieve your long-term goals. They tend to relate to your overarching plans and values. These might include scheduling your workouts, attending continuing education courses, developing relationships with new clients and colleagues, or eating healthy.

Eisenhower helps us sort this out with the matrix he developed (see below). It is a terrific tool that will help you reset your priorities and know where to start.

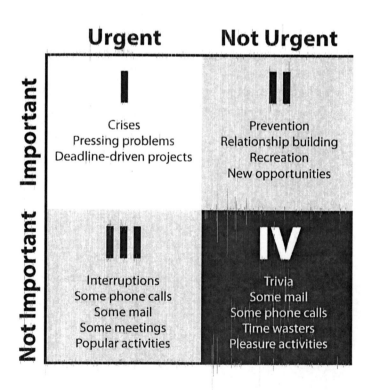

	Urgent	**Not Urgent**
Important	**I** Crises Pressing problems Deadline-driven projects	**II** Prevention Relationship building Recreation New opportunities
Not Important	**III** Interruptions Some phone calls Some mail Some meetings Popular activities	**IV** Trivia Some mail Some phone calls Time wasters Pleasure activities

After you have studied the Eisenhower Matrix, look at your tasks and place them in one of the four categories. Based on how you classify them, you can focus on your work in a way that increases your productivity and brings order to your life.

1. *Important and urgent:* Act immediately.

2. *Important but not urgent:* Schedule the task for when it can be completed at optimal performance.

3. *Urgent but not important:* Delegate these tasks.

4. *Not urgent and not important:* Remove from task list.

The more you use the matrix the better you will be at prioritizing your work and the more productive you will become.

CHAPTER 13

BOUNDARIES AGAINST BURNOUT

My client was almost in tears.

"I'm so overwhelmed that I need to take Xanax to calm myself down. I just don't know how to stop working," the client said. "I work all the time: late at night, on weekends. I don't have kids and if I don't have other family commitments, I feel an expectation to keep working."

I often meet with clients who have worked themselves into a state of burnout. Professionals easily get trapped in a vicious cycle of marketing, getting new clients, delivering the work, following up—rinse and repeat, every day, every week.

I also see this with the healthcare professionals I coach. Their level of responsibility is enormous. They often work in life and death circumstances. They are required to stay abreast of new medical research and manage the financial and personnel aspects of their practices. Although they are expected to handle anything that comes at them, doctors and nurses often face severe professional burnout.

A prominent surgeon (whose name I won't reveal) was called to develop a new health program at a hospital while also sustaining his regular surgery schedule. In order to implement the program, he often had to stay in the hospital for thirty-six hours without sleep.

Then the situation got worse. His partner had to step down from his position due to health problems, which meant that the surgeon had to work on his normal days off. On top of that, a close relative died. He was required to work so much that he couldn't mourn and grieve with the rest of his family. He felt guilty for not being able to help his family in a time of need.

As the situation worsened, his co-workers began to notice behavior and attitude changes. Emergency room doctors complained that he was not responding fast enough. Nurses told his supervisors that he was grouchy and short-fused. He struggled to make simple decisions and left problems unresolved. In response, the hospital administration warned him to shape up, giving him a slap on the wrist. That only made matters worse, adding even more stress.

As the pressure increased, the surgeon became

more anxious. Insomnia became a problem, which in turn left him more tired than ever. As he slogged through his days, his anger and frustration boiled.

He finally blew up. During an operation, the surgeon threw medical instruments around the operating room and yelled at the other doctors and nurses. The hospital administration suspended him and sent him to a therapy center for evaluation.

Everything about the surgeon's troubled behavior and attitudes pointed to the classic symptoms of professional burnout. But even in a hospital environment, he lacked the attention and care he needed. Sadly, all of this could have been avoided had people noticed what was going on in the doctor's life.

This story tells us that humans have limits—both physical and emotional. Unfortunately, corporate culture often fails to take these limits into consideration. We also feel pressured to drive *ourselves* beyond what is human, often because we're afraid of losing our jobs. Then, when workers begin to show signs of burnout, corporations fail to identify ways to help before everything unravels.

It's very easy to go from intense stress at work to burnout. But what does that mean? How do you know if you are on the verge of burnout?

The symptoms of burnout include shear exhaustion, both mentally and physically, combined with an extreme sense of being overwhelmed. Common daily tasks become exasperating and larger-than-life. People notice that your patience is gone and that your temper easily flares. You feel unhappy with your work and lack hope for a better future. Depression combined with increased anxiety can take hold. That can lead to insomnia. Because our bodies are inseparable from our emotions, burnout can lead to chronic pain, heart palpitations, chest pain, and dry mouth. (In these cases, seeking help from a doctor is important.) When you get to the point of burnout, you lose sight of yourself and what makes you happy.

People who wind up in a place of severe burnout have to take dramatic steps to recalibrate and get back to a balanced life. Fortunately, there is hope!

When I meet with clients who are seriously distressed and on the verge of burnout, the first question I ask is, "What do you want?" My client, mentioned at the start of this chapter (let's call him Brent), first answered this question by telling me what he *didn't* want, which was to not feel so overwhelmed all the time. That wasn't a valid answer to my question, so I asked again: "What do you want?" Finally, he said that he wanted to be off work most days at 5 p.m. and, as he had his own law practice, that he wanted to take Fridays off.

That answer was our launching point toward a solution. Knowing what you want makes it easier to build a plan around achieving it. You just need to figure out the obstacles and find solutions.

So I asked Brent what kept him from leaving work at 5 p.m. or taking Fridays off. He told me that he was afraid his clients would leave him if he wasn't always available and responsive.

I told him that words like "afraid" and "fearful" are often signs that the inner critic is spouting off. We say to ourselves: "I'm afraid that if I take one hour a day to be alone or exercise my family will feel abandoned." Or, "I'm afraid to tell a family member about my policy not to coach friends or family because they might not love me anymore." You get the idea.

The truth is that we are usually full of nonsense when we tell ourselves these stories. Believing these lies is what holds us back from setting the healthy boundaries we need to live productive and balanced lives.

In my work with Brent, we decided to develop

ways to tell prospective clients right up front about his work schedule. This way they would know about his work boundaries in a transparent way.

Now Brent explains to clients that his area of law is highly specialized and therefore requires extensive study and concentration. He tells them that when he is working on a case, he usually doesn't answer his phone or email immediately. He says that he always responds by the end of each day, but that urgent matters should be directed to his paralegal first.

He also informs his clients that in order to sustain a healthy life balance he usually ends his work at 5 p.m. and takes Fridays off. Doing this helps him clear his head and enables him to focus better on his cases. This means that he can give 100 percent attention to each client during his working hours. Once his clients agree to his scheduling boundaries, which they all do, he writes these terms into a letter of engagement.

Slowly but surely, Brent has been able to rebuild his schedule with healthy balances. His clients have said how much they respect the fact that he knows how to focus on maintaining a good life balance.

Setting boundaries is the best way to manage your schedule. You first have to identify what specific balance of work and free time you want. Then you have to develop a plan and overcome your inner critic. Finally, execute the plan! At first it might feel uncomfortable, but the more you do it, the easier it gets.

CHAPTER 14

DELEGATE!

WE ALL WISH THAT SOME OF OUR WORK could be done by others. But many business leaders are hesitant to delegate work because they distrust employees or think they are the only ones who can do the job right.

One of my clients (let's call him Rob) is a C-level executive at a Big Four accounting firm. We started working together because he was completely overwhelmed with his workload. The first question I asked him was, "Do you have an executive assistant?"

His answer was, "Yes, but . . ."

"OK," I replied, "Yes, but what?"

"She doesn't do what I ask her to do the way I want it to be done," he said. "She interrupts me with questions when she should know what to do. I find it's easier to do it myself."

He went on and on like this.

I hear the same thing from my clients all the time. The problem usually isn't with the assistant; more of-

ten than not, the problem originates with the delegator. One reason is that time management isn't usually
addressed at business schools, which means that many
leaders aren't trained to delegate in productive ways.

Delegating is one of the most important skills
needed to become a thought leader, visionary, and
strategist. Leaving other important work to a trusted
employee, contractor, or freelancer enables leaders to
focus on business growth and new opportunities. This
chapter will help you become a "rock star" delegator.

My favorite delegator is Richard Branson, founder
of the Virgin Group, which includes more than four
hundred companies. He frequently shares his tips for
success. One that has stayed in my mind for years is:
"You need to learn to delegate so that you can focus
on the big picture." When we get stuck focusing on
small details we are not able to make long-range plans,
pay attention to market trends, or think about how to
improve our companies. Moreover, when we're over-
run by details, our stress increases, our productivity de-
creases, and our work-life balance unravels.

If you are a small-business owner, chances are
you have done everything by yourself for many years.
This probably means that it's been difficult for you to

achieve greater goals. You simply run out of capacity.

Even senior executives get caught in this do-it-all-yourself web. One of the most powerful chief executives, President Jimmy Carter, was known to be a stickler for small details. In fact, it was reported that he would schedule who could play on the White House tennis courts. I also read that he would type a list of music selections to be played in the executive mansion.

When you get caught in these weeds, it might send a message to your staff that they cannot be trusted to do the work. It discourages them. And, as we will see, employees lose the opportunity to grow and improve professionally when business leaders refuse to delegate.

The challenge is to delegate well.

DECIDE WHAT TASKS TO DELEGATE

First get clarity about all the tasks you should or should not delegate. As a small-business owner, you might be doing your own bookkeeping. When you focus on that during your work day, you are actually losing billable hours. Instead, consider outsourcing those services to a professional. There are thousands of freelancers and contractors who specialize in services that you usually do yourself, especially if you are a small-business owner. If you can get back to what you are most passionate about and best at then you will be more likely to see your business grow.

Are you a trained web designer? If not, but you still insist on designing your own site, then you might end up sifting through a million blogs just to do something that would be simple for a professional. It would be more cost and time effective to hire a web designer.

Take an audit of your abilities and responsibilities. What can you delegate? Travel planning, editing, writing, expense reports, PowerPoint presentations, hiring new staff members, competitive research? If you do not have an executive assistant, I recommend finding freelancers. Let's look next at some ideas to help you think more clearly about delegating.

Delegate routine tasks. If you understand these tasks and know what outcome you want, then it will be easy to communicate your objectives to your employees.

Delegate work that requires skills you don't have. Learning new skills might be beneficial, but trying to learn everything takes time. If your employees have the right skills to do the work, hand it over to them.

Delegate tasks that don't have immediate deadlines. Researching materials for blogs, newsletters, and reports that pertain to your business are all good examples. Establish a deadline so your employees know when each task is due.

Delegate responsibilities to talented employees. If you have an employee that has a degree in a certain area or expertise from past work experience, then give that person an opportunity to show you what they can do.

Delegate to help employees develop skills. If you have an employee who wants to grow in his or her career, then give them tasks that will help them develop. A new skill will benefit them and your company.

PREPARATION, COMMUNICATION, AND PLANNING

Once you have clarity about what to delegate, then it's up to you, the manager, to make sure you delegate and communicate effectively. Delegating requires preparation. It takes a lot more than just dropping some documents on your assistant's desk and mumbling a few words about a deadline as you walk by. No, you need to be constructive and thoughtful. Take the act of delegating seriously, because it will have a great impact on you and your organization.

First, explain the whole picture so that the person understands the importance of the tasks and how they fit into the overall project. It helps people when they can see the whole picture of a jigsaw puzzle before they start working on specific projects.

Second, explain in detail what you want done and what the final product should look like. In other words, make sure that your assistants understand what you expect from them. But remember: Rarely will a person work exactly like you, so appreciate each person's unique approach.

Third, give constructive feedback to your employees if something doesn't meet expectations. Feedback is essential to training. You will do yourself and your assistants a disservice if you don't give feedback and direction at the end of every task or project. Communicating feedback is not about negative criticism. Identify what worked well, not just the areas that can be corrected or changed the next time around. Remember that people make mistakes. Give them a chance. Provide encouraging feedback as to how they can improve. Don't demean them. This way you won't create an uncomfortable work environment.

Fourth, establish clear deadlines for each project. I frequently hear executive assistants say they get called to the carpet for not getting something done on time.

But I soon learn that the executive didn't communicate the deadline very well. As a delegator, you must set a deadline for every step of the project and make sure everyone knows when tasks are due.

Fifth, establish a schedule for short progress updates. If your assistants provide you with weekly progress reports, you will have confidence that the work is getting done. You'll also give employees an opportunity to ask questions. Use a worksheet or project management software to track progress.

Sixth, find the right balance for the autonomy you give your assistants. If you assign a task that requires an employee to spend money, make sure to establish a budget so that they don't have to keep running to you for approval. Giving employees autonomy within clear budget parameters will increase efficiency for you and your employee. However, use discernment when giving autonomy to employees when a project involves, for example, sensitive information. When you entrust an employee with sensitive material, make sure that others involved in the project are aware of your decision.

Finally, don't be the one to hold up the progress of a project. It is easy to get busy and, as a result, fail to respond to the needs of your assistants. Delays in your participation can cause ripple effects in the schedules of others on your team.

Delegating will increase your personal capacity, your organization's effectiveness, and your employees' professional development. Most importantly, smart delegating will enable you to focus on what matters most for the future of your business and career.

AUTHOR'S NOTE

OUR TIME IS PRECIOUS, BUT IT'S ELUSIVE. After raising kids, parents can find themselves looking at their adult children and say, "Where did the time go?" Or we might look in the mirror, find a new wrinkle or another gray hair and say, "When did that happen?"

This book was written to help you manage your time in order to maximize the fullness of your life. I don't want anyone to look back and wonder where the time went. By practicing the techniques offered in *Own Your Time,* you will be able to say that you lived intentionally, and that your life was productive and balanced. The people in your life will thank you for the time you invested in them.

As an executive coach and business owner, I know that professionals are under tremendous stress and time constraints. And I recognize that we can't control our time all the time. I was once sent on a very important assignment just as I was preparing to leave on a three-week family vacation. Needless to say, I felt stuck, sad, and disappointed.

Interruptions like that can and do happen. The key is to maintain a balance so that you are not dependent on just an annual vacation to spend time with family and friends. When life is balanced, you can spend time caring for yourself and enjoying the company of those you love *frequently,* not just once a year. Taking control of your time will result in a full life without regrets.

I know from experience that finding a balance is a daily challenge, but by doing small things every day to win back your time you will live with a focus on what is most important to you.

As you develop your time-management abilities, I highly recommend working with a coach. Having someone at your side goes a long way toward building new habits. You can find resources on my website (www.stephaniewachman.com), and you can seek out an accountability partner in a friend or family member to help you stay on track.

My heart-felt desire is that you find success in owning your time and relief in this high-pressured life.